The River Raft Dash

Written by Alison Milford

Illustrated by Gustavo Mazali

RISING STARS

Oscar, Anna and Blair had waited all year for the Summer River Fair.

Anna pointed at the fluttering banners.
"They must be for the fair," she said.

Blair went to look at a banner.

Join the
River Raft Dash

"I wish Mum and I had a raft," she sighed.
"We can help!" said Oscar.

The children got some logs.
They secured them with string.

Then they added a silver tinfoil dragon with a coiled tail.

Have this thicker string.

There were lots of rafts for the River Raft Dash.

As the rafts turned the corner, Oscar said,
"I can hear thunder!"

Soon Blair and her mum were near
the end.
"We are going to win!" said Blair.

Then the rain began to spoil the river dash.

Blair's mum was not sure how to get near the raft.

Blair flung the coiled string across the river. The rafts were joined.

Thank you!

The crowd clapped when the pair of rafts got back.
A tear ran down Anna's cheek!

Blair did not win the River Raft Dash
but she was still given a medal.

Best
Helper

Talk about the story

Ask your child these questions:

1 What was the name of the race?

2 What was the silver dragon made from?

3 Why did Anna have a tear on her cheek?

4 Why do you think Blair was given a medal?

5 Is there a river near where you live? What is it called?

6 If you had to build a raft, what would it look like?

Can your child retell the story in their own words?